■ BRITISH HISTORY MAKERS ■

QUEEN VICTORIA

LEON ASHWORTH

CHERRYTREE BOOKS

A Cherrytree Book

Designed and produced by
A S Publishing

First published 1997
by Cherrytree Press Ltd
a subsidiary of
The Chivers Company Ltd
Windsor Bridge Road
Bath BA2 3AX

British Library Cataloguing in Publication Data

Ashworth, Leon
    Queen Victoria. – (British history makers)
    1. Victoria, Queen of Great Britain – Juvenile literature
    2. Queens – Great Britain – Juvenile literature
    3. Great Britain – Kings and rulers – Juvenile literature
    4. Great Britain – History – Victoria, 1837-1901 –
        Juvenile literature
    I. Title
    941'.081'092

ISBN 0 7451 5291 0 (Hardcover)
ISBN 0 7540 9014 0 (Softcover)

Printed and bound in Italy by New Interlitho, Milan

Acknowledgments

Design: Richard Rowan
Editorial: John Grisewood
Artwork: Malcolm Porter
Photographs: *The Bridgeman Art Library* Cover portrait, 4 bottom left (Forbes
Magazine Collection), 8/9 bottom Victoria & Albert Museum), 10/11 bottom
(Forbes Magazine Collection), 12/13 bottom (Christie's Images), 13 bottom right
(Victoria & Albert Museum), 16 bottom & front cover (Royal Holloway &
Bedford New College), 18 bottom (Stapleton Collection), 19 top (Stapleton
Collection), 20 bottom (Patrimonio Nacional, Madrid), 20/21 top (Forbes
Magazine Collection) 22 bottom (British Library), 24 top (Scottish
National Portrait Gallery, Edinburgh), 26/27 top (Private Collection), 27
bottom (Trustees of the Weston Park Foundation), 28 bottom (Guildhall
Art Gallery) *Chester Toy Museum* 9 centre *Hulton Getty* 14 bottom left *The
Hutchison Library* 28/29 top *Mary Evans Picture Library* 5, 8 bottom left, 9 top
& bottom right, 10 bottom left, 12 left, top & centre, 14/15 top, 15 right top
& bottom, 16/17 top, 18 top, 19 bottom, 21 right, 22 top, 23 top left &
bottom, 25 top & bottom, 26 centre & bottom, 27 centre, 29 left centre
& bottom, bottom centre *Public Record Office* 4 centre *Royal Collection* ©
Her Majesty the Queen 6, 7, 10/11 top, 14/15 bottom, 17 bottom (& back
cover), 24 bottom *Zefa* 23 right centre, 29 bottom right

CONTENTS

VICTORIA – MOTHER OF THE EMPIRE 4

BORN TO BE QUEEN 6

ROYAL PRINCESS 8

QUEEN AND CROWNED 10

WIFE AND MOTHER 12

THE ROYAL FAMILY 14

HOME AND ABROAD 16

THE GREAT EXHIBITION 18

WAR IN THE CRIMEA 20

THE DEATH OF ALBERT 22

WIDOW 24

EMPRESS OF INDIA 26

THE VICTORIAN AGE 28

GLOSSARY 30

PLACES TO VISIT 31

INDEX 32

■ Victoria — Mother of the Empire

VICTORIA WAS queen of the United Kingdom of Great Britain and Ireland for more than 60 years – longer than any other British monarch. This small woman who reigned over the vast British empire gave her name to the Victorian age.

The kings who ruled before Victoria (William IV and George IV) had become figures of fun, jeered at by crowds in the street. Respect for the monarch was at a low ebb. Victoria came to the throne as a young girl, knowing little of government. She undertook her new duties with determination and from her beloved husband Albert she learned a high sense of duty. Her people saw that she was dedicated to her role, and loved her for it.

Victoria could not play a part in politics – deciding on new laws – as earlier monarchs had. That power had shifted to the prime minister and parliament. But the queen became a person of enormous authority, and not just at court. She was admired throughout the world, becoming the

▲ Victoria's signature – *Victoria Reg* (*Reg* being short for *Regina*, the Latin for 'Queen').

◀ The young queen painted by the fashionable German portrait artist Franz Xavier Winterhalter.

VICTORIA'S LIFE

1819 Victoria born
1837 Becomes queen
1840 Marries Prince Albert
1851 Great Exhibition
1854 Crimean War
1861 Prince Albert dies
1876 Named Empress of India
1887 Celebrates Golden Jubilee
1897 Celebrates Diamond Jubilee
1899 Boer War
1901 Victoria dies

▶ Steamships, railways, electric light and the motor car were all invented during Victoria's reign.

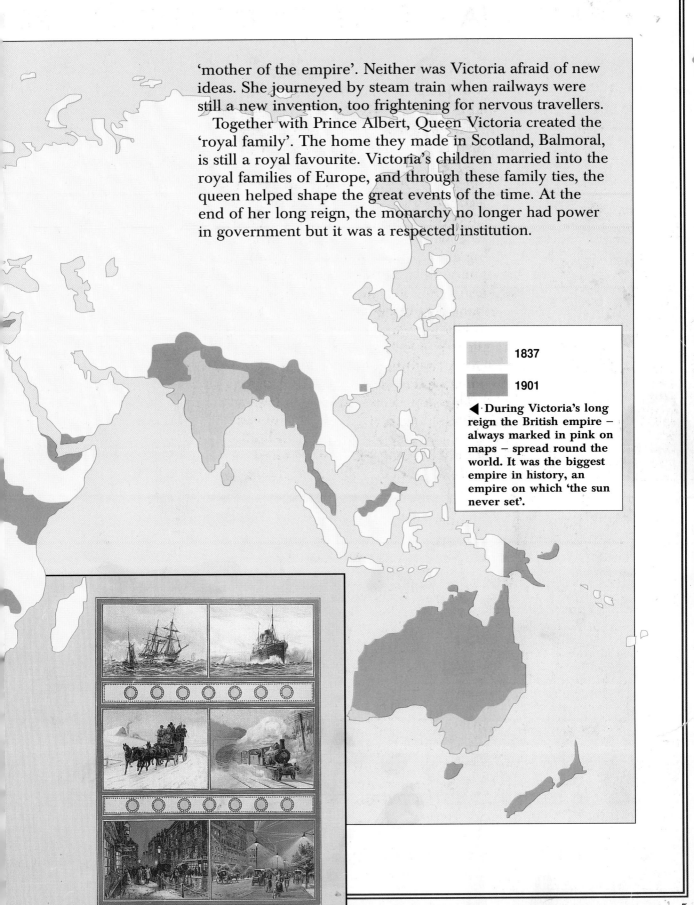

'mother of the empire'. Neither was Victoria afraid of new ideas. She journeyed by steam train when railways were still a new invention, too frightening for nervous travellers.

Together with Prince Albert, Queen Victoria created the 'royal family'. The home they made in Scotland, Balmoral, is still a royal favourite. Victoria's children married into the royal families of Europe, and through these family ties, the queen helped shape the great events of the time. At the end of her long reign, the monarchy no longer had power in government but it was a respected institution.

	1837
	1901

◄ During Victoria's long reign the British empire – always marked in pink on maps – spread round the world. It was the biggest empire in history, an empire on which 'the sun never set'.

■ BORN TO BE QUEEN ■

O N 24 MAY 1819, a baby girl was born at Kensington Palace in London. Her father was the Duke of Kent, the king's son. Her mother was a German princess. Her grandfather, King George III, was old and ill. There were few children in the British royal family. It was quite possible that, one day, the baby might be queen.

A FAMILY QUARREL

The new parents were delighted with their daughter and chose names for her christening. But at this event there was a family row. The child's uncle George behaved so badly that he made her mother cry. He demanded that the baby be named Alexandrina Victoria – and so she was. George was the prince regent, acting as king in place of his sick father.

KINGS WITHOUT CHILDREN

The next year, when George III died, the prince regent became King George IV. He reigned for ten years, before his brother came to the throne as William IV. Neither king had any children to succeed him. Victoria's father had died when

VICTORIA'S RELATIONS

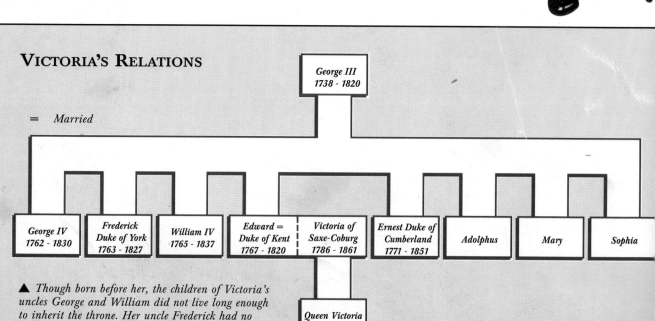

= Married

```
                          George III
                          1738 - 1820

George IV    Frederick     William IV    Edward =      Victoria of   Ernest Duke of   Adolphus   Mary   Sophia
1762 - 1830  Duke of York  1765 - 1837   Duke of Kent  Saxe-Coburg   Cumberland
             1763 - 1827                 1767 - 1820   1786 - 1861   1771 - 1851

                                              Queen Victoria
                                              1819 - 1901
```

▲ *Though born before her, the children of Victoria's uncles George and William did not live long enough to inherit the throne. Her uncle Frederick had no children. George III had more sons and daughters, not shown on the chart. In all he had 15 children.*

Victoria's father, Edward, Duke of Kent, was the fourth son of George III. In 1818 he married Princess Maria Louisa Victoria of Saxe-Coburg. He died eight months after the birth of their child, Victoria.

▼ The Duchess of Kent with her two-year-old daughter, Princess Victoria, at home in Kensington Palace. The young princess was lively but quick-tempered and she was brought up simply and strictly.

she was only eight months old, and little Drina (as the princess was known until she was nine) seemed more likely than ever to be the next British queen.

A CHANGING WORLD

The child had been born into a fast-changing world. She was the first member of the royal family to be vaccinated against the dreaded disease of smallpox – thanks to the discovery of vaccination by Dr Edward Jenner in 1796. Many more discoveries made during Victoria's long life were to have a profound effect on ordinary people.

The little princess was soon introduced to the world. Her soldier father took her to her first military parade when she was only three months old. She was to watch many, many more.

■ ROYAL PRINCESS ■

THE LITTLE PRINCESS lived in London at Kensington Palace with her mother and half-sister Feodore. She had a nurse to look after her and a German governess called Lehzen. Until she was three, Victoria spoke only German. She saw little of her English uncles, but enjoyed visiting her mother's brother Leopold, who kept an eye on the family and lent them money.

Life in the nursery was lonely and dull, Victoria later complained. Outside, the London streets were lively enough. People were quick to gather in crowds to protest about the government and politics, and sometimes the mob turned violent and there were riots.

A LUCKY ESCAPE

The princess was looked after with great care, yet accidents did happen. While she was sleeping in her cot, a boy shooting birds smashed her nursery window and stray shotgun pellets ripped through her nightdress. Later, she had to hold somebody's hand when she walked downstairs and she was never left alone. The Duchess of Kent and her daughter slept in the same bedroom until Victoria became queen. Although governess Lehzen was strict, the princess adored her. She did not, however, like Sir John Conroy, who controlled her mother's business affairs.

EVENTS

1826 *Fenimore Cooper's story* Last of the Mohicans *is published. Victoria later reads it. First true photograph is made.*
1829 *Sir Robert Peel starts London's first organized police force, nicknamed 'Peelers' or 'Bobbies'. Louis Braille invents a reading system for the blind. The waltz is popular.*
1830 *King George IV dies.*
1831 *King William IV is crowned. Leopold becomes first king of Belgium. Michael Faraday discovers how to make electricity drive machines.*
1835 *Victoria tours the north of England.*

▶ Nursery life for the young princess was dull. She had no friends like these to play horse with.

GOING TO SCHOOL

WHEN VICTORIA was a child, there was no free schooling for all. Boys from rich families were often sent away to school, but girls and some boys were taught lessons at home by tutors. Charles Dickens' story *Nicholas Nickleby* (1838) describes a school where boys are treated terribly. There were also small church schools and 'dame schools', like this one, which were often housed in the teacher's home. Sunday schools had been started in 1780, to teach adults as well as children. In 1820, 'ragged schools' began giving free lessons to poor children, but primary schooling for all children did not start until 1870.

▼ From the age of four, Victoria had lessons at home. She learnt French, German, drawing and

'I WILL BE GOOD'

When she was seven, Victoria had a holiday at Windsor Castle with her uncle, King George IV. There were parties, music and dancing. Two years later, her sister Feodore left home to marry, and in 1831 her uncle Leopold left England to become king of the Belgians. By this time, Victoria had realized that one day she would be queen and had at once declared 'I will be good'.

CHILDREN'S TOYS

VICTORIA loved dolls. She and Lehzen dressed 132 wooden puppets as characters from favourite operas or stories by Sir Walter Scott. Children of the time played with dolls' shops, houses and prams, toy soldiers made of wood, tin or lead, and toy pistols. There were hoops, tops, balls, and clockwork toys that moved. Kaleidoscopes were new playthings, invented in 1816. On Sunday, toys were locked away in many households. Only a Noah's Ark collection of figures from the Bible story was allowed for play.

piano. She was good at arithmetic but found Latin hard. Most of all she loved to sing and dance.

▶ 'I see I am nearer the throne than I supposed,' declared the 12-year-old princess Victoria when she discovered during a history lesson that one day she might be queen. Realizing this, she made the promise 'I will be good'.

■ QUEEN AND CROWNED ■

V ICTORIA'S MOTHER wanted the people to see her daughter. When she was 13, the princess visited the Midlands and Wales. The tour was tiring, with 5am starts, but Victoria saw for the first time the new industrial Britain. 'I just now see an extraordinary building flaming with fire,' she wrote in her diary. She was looking at the furnace of an ironworks. She also learned how working people lived. 'The men, women, children, country and houses are all black.' Families lived in small, badly built houses, worked long hours in factories and mines, and often went hungry.

HOME LIFE AND PETS

A year later, Victoria was in Portsmouth to see Admiral Nelson's ship *Victory*. She ate beef and potatoes, like the sailors, and drank rum. On such visits, and on holidays, Victoria painted and wrote her diary. She loved animals and riding her pony, Rosa. When her mother was given a spaniel called Dash, Victoria adopted it. She dressed the dog in a red jacket with blue trousers. She also kept a parakeet and a canary.

EVENTS

1835 *Hans Christian Andersen's children's stories are published in Denmark. In South Africa, Boer (Dutch) farmers begin the Great Trek to find new lands, fighting Zulus as they go.*
1836 *Naturalist Charles Darwin returns home in* HMS Beagle *after a five-year voyage of scientific research.*
1838 *Victoria is crowned. The newest best-selling book is* Oliver Twist, *by Charles Dickens. First steamships cross the Atlantic Ocean.*

▲ **Eighteen-year-old Victoria greets the archbishop of Canterbury and the lord chamberlain at 5am on 20 June 1837 as they tell her the news that she is queen.**

◀ **'Please sir, I want some more'. An illustration by George Cruikshank of Oliver asking for more food in Charles Dickens' best-selling, serial novel *Oliver Twist*. Victoria greatly enjoyed the book. Its descriptions of poverty and workhouse life shocked the public.**

ILLNESS AND A CHEERING VISIT

In 1835, Victoria was very ill with typhoid fever. During her long recovery, she spent much time knitting. The next year, for her 17th birthday, her cousins Ernest and Albert came on a visit from Germany. Victoria found Albert 'delightful'. He was nearly her own age, made everyone laugh and played happily with Dash.

THE KING IS DEAD . . .

At this time, Victoria and her mother were not on good terms. They quarrelled over Sir John Conroy. King William asked for the princess to spend more time at court, but Victoria was kept away. The king wanted Victoria to marry one of her English cousins, but her mother and uncle Leopold had their eyes on Albert as the ideal husband. On 18 May 1837, Victoria legally came of age – she was 18. A month later, King William died.

. . . LONG LIVE THE QUEEN

The news came at dawn. Victoria was now queen. She walked downstairs to greet the archbishop of Canterbury, holding her mother's hand. A few hours later, she met the men who were now her closest advisers, the privy councillors. Among them were Lord Melbourne, the prime minister, the Duke of Wellington, hero of the battle of Waterloo, Sir Robert Peel and Lord Palmerston (both future prime ministers). Victoria spoke and acted as if she had been queen all her life.

The young queen moved to Buckingham Palace, where Dash was happy to play in the garden. On 28 June 1838, Victoria was crowned in Westminster Abbey.

▼ The coronation ceremony was so long that even the prime minister became exhausted. Victoria had more energy. When she got home to the palace she ran to give her pet dog Dash his bath.

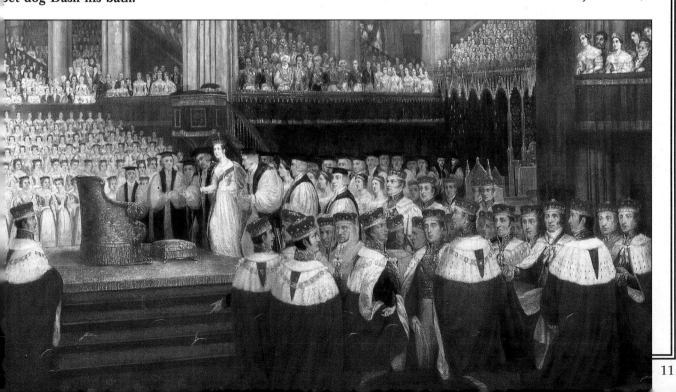

■WIFE AND MOTHER■

THERE WAS SO much to interest the young queen. Lord Melbourne, the prime minister, gave her advice and taught her how the government worked, but he was also an entertaining companion. Victoria came to look on him almost as a father. She was enjoying *Oliver Twist* by Charles Dickens, which was published as a serial. There was so much to do that she sometimes gobbled her food, in her haste.

THE QUEEN PROPOSES

Cousin Albert wrote to congratulate Victoria on her coronation. In October 1839, arrived in Windsor for a visit. The Channel crossing had made him seasick, but Victoria still found him 'beautiful'. She proposed (it was thought improper for Albert to do so, being of lower rank), and the couple were married on 10 February 1840 in the Chapel Royal at St James's Palace in London.

Every piece of the queen's wedding outfit was made in Britain. But Albert

EVENTS

1838 *Troops guard city streets during marches by Chartists (reformers calling for the vote for working people).*
1839 *An electric telegraph service begins in London. First bicycle.*
1840 *First postage stamps – 'penny blacks' – bearing Victoria's head (below).*

With Waitangi treaty, New Zealand becomes a British colony. On a wet February morning, Victoria and Albert are married. Dash, Victoria's pet dog, dies.

▼ **Victoria seated in a carriage with her mother, the Duchess of Kent, in Windsor Great Park. Among those on horseback are Prince Albert, the Duke of Wellington and the future prime minister, Sir Robert Peel.**

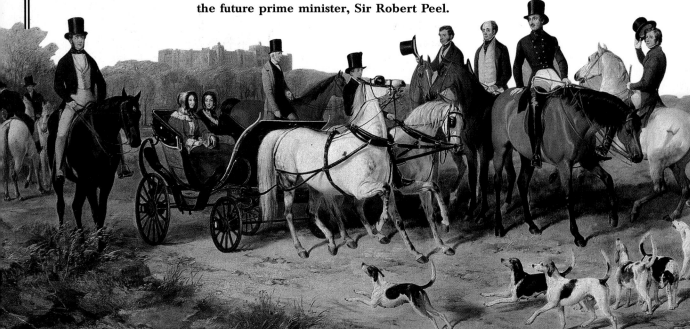

THE HUNGRY FORTIES

ALL OVER Europe, poor workers were calling for change. In Britain, millions of people – called Chartists – signed a petition calling for reform of parliament. There were riots (left) and strikes. Factory workers broke their machines. A group of workers in Rochdale started a self-help scheme and opened the first Co-operative shop. In Ireland in 1846, the potato crop failed and millions went hungry (below). Tens of thousands of Irish people left home and sailed to new lives in America.

was a foreigner and not everyone was happy about the marriage. He was given only a small allowance of money and no title (such as duke). Melbourne explained to Victoria that times were hard. Many people in Britain were out of work and hungry. The country could afford no more.

A MUCH LOVED HUSBAND

Albert was clever, hard-working and well educated. He liked fencing and skating, was interested in science and the arts, and shared with Victoria a love of music. He too had a dog, a black greyhound with a silver streak named Eos (Dawn).

Above all, Albert had a strong sense of duty. Through his example, Victoria learned to be a good monarch. At first, she worked at her government papers alone. 'Albert helped with the blotting paper when I signed.' When she was expecting their first child, Albert began seeing ministers and reading documents. Soon the queen began to depend on his help and advice. Their desks were placed side by side. 'The prince understands everything so well and has a clever, able head,' Lord Melbourne told Victoria.

▶ **The queen and Prince Albert dance the polka. The couple shared a love of music. Since childhood, Victoria had enjoyed theatre visits, especially to see the opera and ballet. Albert wrote music and songs, which the two sang as duets. Victoria's voice was striking: light, clear and 'silvery'. Her movements too were light, graceful and dignified.**

■THE ROYAL FAMILY■

I N JUNE 1840, the queen was expecting her first child. As she rode through London in her carriage one day, a boy raised his cap to her. Then shots rang out. The boy's father seized the gunman, who was later locked up in a lunatic asylum for 27 years. The queen showed great bravery, as she did at other times when her life was in danger. The boy, John Millais, grew up to be a famous painter. The queen's baby, born in November, was a girl – Princess Victoria.

I N VICTORIAN times, couples could not easily limit the size of their families and might have 10 or more children. Giving birth was often dangerous, even though doctors were learning more about germs and diseases.

EVENTS

1840 *On 21 November, Victoria's first child, Princess Victoria Adelaide Mary Louise, is born. The queen's pet name for her is 'Pussy'.*
1842 *Edwin Chadwick reports on the poor state of water supplies and drains in British cities. New laws ban women and children from working underground in coal mines. China leases Hong Kong to Britain.*
1844 *The engineer Isambard Kingdom Brunel launches the* Great Britain, *the largest steamship yet built.*

A SON AND A NEW ADVISER

The Prince of Wales, Albert Edward, was born a year later, in 1841. Victoria now said goodbye to her old governess, Lehzen, who went home to Germany. She also had a new prime minister, Robert Peel, whom she liked – once she got used to him. Peel recognized Albert's abilities, and Albert made Victoria see that in the British system of government, the monarch must not take sides between rival political parties. Albert was proving a good organizer, changing the way the palace was run to save money. He shared the queen's commonsense attitude.

◀ **An excited royal family round the Christmas tree. Prince Albert brought over many customs from Germany, including decorating trees with candles and baubles.**

▶ **The royal family in 1846, shown as home-loving, informal and relaxed. Victoria's secure family life was in sharp contrast to the grinding poverty of many needy working-class families.**

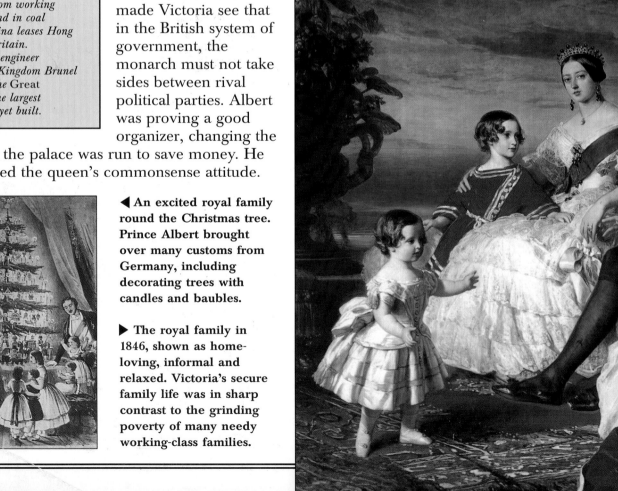

Many mothers and babies (like these from the workhouse) died during childbirth or soon afterwards. Small children might die from measles, whooping cough, tuberculosis or a host of other illnesses. Water supplies – from wells and street pumps – were not always clean. Dirty water caused diseases such as typhoid and cholera.

"CLEANLINESS IS NEXT TO GODLINESS."

▲ Good, clean living was a working-class ideal.

FAMILY CHRISTMAS

Christmas was a merry time, much enjoyed by the queen, who had been lonely as a child. Albert ordered Christmas trees from Germany, and this custom spread through the land. The family rode in horse-sleighs driven by Albert, made snowmen and played ice hockey.

NEW INVENTIONS

FOR THE christening of Princess Helena in 1846, the chapel at Buckingham Palace was lit by gas for the first time. London had had gas lamps since 1807, when Pall Mall was the first street to be gaslit. To light gas lamps at home, people had new safety matches – so much easier than striking a spark from a flint. The baby princess was born just too early to have her nappy fastened with a safety pin – invented in 1849.

■ HOME AND ABROAD ■

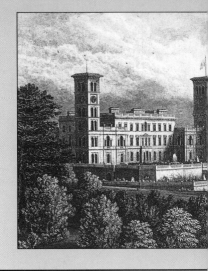

IN 1842, VICTORIA and Albert took their first train ride. 'Not so fast next time, Mr Conductor,' the prince is said to have asked when they arrived at Windsor from Paddington. The queen enjoyed the privacy and speed of the train. Horses had run away and tipped her from her coach more than once and she disliked being peered at by crowds when the coach stopped.

TIME FOR CHANGE

Victoria and Albert bought a holiday home called Osborne on the Isle of Wight and the prince replanned it for their growing family. By 1848, Victoria had six children, the youngest being Princess Louise. She had three more babies, the last two born with the aid of anaesthetics – a new invention to ease pain.

At Windsor and Buckingham Palace, builders were at work improving the smelly drains and lavatories. Everyone feared outbreaks of cholera, a disease now known to be spread by unclean water. The builders also added a balcony to the front of Buckingham Palace.

Prime minister Peel and Albert taught Victoria about the social problems of the day. These were

EVENTS

1844 *Vulcanized rubber is invented.*
1846 *Potato crop fails, causing mass famine in Ireland. First use of ether as a painkiller. Discovery of the planet Neptune.*
1847 *Victoria enjoys her first sea bathe, but dislikes putting her head under water.*
1848 *Gold rush in California, USA. Revolutions in France, Austria-Hungary, Italy and Germany. The queen strongly disapproves of revolutions.*
1849 *A London doctor, John Snow, proves that boiling drinking water lessens the risk of catching cholera. An Irishman tries to shoot Victoria with a home-made pistol. The following year (1850) a retired army officer hits her on the head while she drives in her carriage!*

SMOKE AND STEAM

EARLY in 1837, Victoria saw her first train. 'We saw the steam carriage pass . . . striking sparks as it flew along the railroad, enveloped in clouds of smoke & making a loud noise. It is a curious thing indeed!'

The railway age had begun in 1825 with the opening of the Stockton and Darlington line, the first public steam railway. Britain led the world in the new

▼ **Bustle and excitement at Paddington Station. A dog is put on a lead; a mother kisses her son goodbye; police arrest a suspect.**

SCOTLAND AND THE ISLE OF WIGHT

IN 1848, the royal family first went to Balmoral – 'a pretty little castle' – in Scotland. Scotland's mountains and forests reminded Albert of Germany, and he and Victoria liked the Highland people. The prince hunted and fished, and tried to learn Gaelic. The family took to Scottish country dancing and even wore kilts. Victoria and Albert also owned a holiday home called Osborne (left) on the Isle of Wight.

troubled times. Revolution had sent the king of France into exile in England. Might Britain too face a revolt? The queen was kind-hearted and wanted help given to the poor. She was horrified to hear of the famine in Ireland, but had no time for reformers like the Chartists, who marched through the streets with their petitions demanding political reforms.

GETTING AWAY FROM IT ALL

In 1843, the royal couple took a sea trip to Scotland and holidayed in France – the first visit to France by a reigning monarch since Henry VIII in 1520. In Belgium, the writer Charlotte Brontë saw the queen in the street and noted her laughing – and her plain dress. Victoria had a loud laugh, and she was often amused – despite her reputation for solemnity.

Victoria and Albert liked a cosy domestic life better than grand palaces. At Osborne, Albert built a beach hut on their small sandy beach. Here the queen undressed in a bathing machine (a hut on wheels that was dragged into the water) and took her first sea bathe in 1847. Some of her subjects began to do the same. Seaside holidays had been made possible by the railways, which gave fast, cheap travel from the industrial towns.

...chnology, and new railway ...acks were being built across ...e country. By 1870, over ...0,000 kilometres of track ...nked major towns and ports.

1870

Cheap rail travel transformed ...eople's lives. Trips to the ...easide became popular. Resorts ...uch as Ramsgate grew rapidly. ...ven when it was sunny, people ...tayed well covered.

■ THE GREAT EXHIBITION ■

ALBERT WAS BUSY with plans for a great festival of science and industry. Called the Great Exhibition, it was to open on 1 May 1851 inside the world's biggest glass building, the Crystal Palace. Many opponents ridiculed the scheme, but the prince pressed on with it for two years, with the total support of his wife.

EVENTS

1849 The Prince of Wales has his first tutor, but his parents are not happy with his progress.
1850 Robert Peel and William Wordsworth (the country's most famous poet) die.
1851 Gold rush in Australia. Great Exhibition opens in London. Louis Napoleon seizes power in France. Alfred Tennyson is made Poet Laureate.
1852 Duke of Wellington dies.
1853 Sir George Cayley tests a man-carrying glider. Fire breaks out in the dining-room at Windsor Castle. The queen is one of the first women to have 'that blessed chloroform' as a painkiller when Prince Leopold is born.

A GOOD LIFE

The exhibition was to celebrate peace between nations, free trade between countries (a matter of great argument at the time) and the progress of science. It was also to honour honest toil. Facing the Crystal Palace in London's Hyde Park, Albert had some 'ideal homes' for working families built for visitors to see.

The Great Exhibition was opened by the queen on 'the happiest day of my life'. She wore the glittering Koh-i-Noor diamond, from India, on a silver and pink dress, and appeared before cheering crowds on the new balcony at Buckingham Palace – the start of a royal tradition.

▲ An ideal kitchen for a working family. The coal-fired range heated the food and the room. It had an oven on one side and a hot-water boiler on the other.

▼ For the Great Exhibition, Joseph Paxton designed a vast structure of cast iron and glass. The Crystal Palace was like a giant greenhouse, tall enough to enclose trees growing in Hyde Park, where it was built.

▲ People marvelled at the exhibits from overseas. The Indian display included fine silks, carpets and canopies, and an ornately dressed stuffed elephant.

A HUGE SUCCESS

Over the next 140 days, six million visitors came to the exhibition from all over Britain, from Europe, America and other parts of the world. The queen went nearly every day, until she left for the Isle of Wight in July. She saw many 'wonders and novelties', including Indian pearls, knives made of Sheffield steel, locks, the electric telegraph, even a machine for making 50,000 medals a week.

GROWING FAST

THE NUMBER of people in Britain was growing rapidly. There were about 15.5 million people in 1800. There were 27 million by the time of the Great Exhibition in 1851. In 1800, most people lived and worked in the countryside. Now Britain was an industrial nation, and most of its people lived in towns. London was by far the largest city, with more than a million people. Many city dwellers lived in squalid slum housing with no piped water. To cope with the extra people, town councils had to set up police and fire services, schools and hospitals.

▲ The pollution from industry was so great that parts of the Midlands became known as the Black Country.

■ WAR IN THE CRIMEA ■

I N 1854, THE QUEEN wrote in her diary: 'The year opens gloomily'. War between the Turks and the Russians had begun. Britain and France were soon sending troops to the Crimea, near the Black Sea, to help the Turks.

Britain and France feared that Russia was growing too strong, and might threaten their own trade and possessions in the Middle East and Asia. Victoria and Albert had tried to keep Britain out of the war. But when her troopships set off, Victoria waved them goodbye.

WAR BROUGHT HOME

The Crimean War was the first war in which newspaper stories and pictures came from reporters on the spot. For the first time, people at home saw photographs of war. The news stories told a sorry tale – of mistakes by army generals, supplies going astray and sickness in the soldiers' camps. More soldiers were dying of disease than were being killed in battle.

Florence Nightingale took 38 nurses to the Crimea to set up a hospital. The

EVENTS

1853 David Livingstone sets out on a three-year journey on foot across Africa.

1854 Battles of Inkerman and Balaclava in the Crimea. Charge of the Light Brigade. Commodore Perry of the US Navy forces Japan to open its ports to Western trade.

1855 Livingstone sees the waterfall he names Victoria Falls. Henry Bessemer invents a way to make steel in huge amounts.

1856 Louis Pasteur discovers that disease is spread by germs in the air.

THE START OF MODERN NURSING

B EFORE the Crimean War, there were no nurses as we know them. There were no women doctors either. There were women midwives and home nurses, but nursing was not thought a fit profession for respectable women. Florence Nightingale became famous for

RUSSIA

CRIMEA

Sevastopol × Inkerman
× Balaclava

Black Sea

...aking up her work in the Crimea. In 1860, she set up the first school for nurses, in St Thomas's Hospital in London. Queen Victoria laid the foundation stone. Hospitals were becoming cleaner, safer places thanks to the discovery of antiseptics to kill germs.

▲ **Florence Nightingale receiving wounded soldiers at Scutari in Turkey in 1856.**

◀ **The position of the Crimea on the Black Sea.**

▼ **The charge of the Light Brigade – at Balaclava on 25 October 1854 – was a military bungle resulting in a tragic loss of lives.**

army commanders did not want her, but the wounded men could not thank her enough, and the queen gave her support. Albert urged the government to send help to the troops more quickly. He worked out ways to reform the army. Victoria sent woolly mittens and scarves to the soldiers and she wrote letters to widows whose husbands had been killed. She visited the wounded when they were brought home to hospitals in Britain.

When peace came in 1856, Victoria watched the returning troops parade past as she sat on horseback, wearing army uniform. She gave out medals: 'Many of the privates (ordinary soldiers) smiled . . . all touched my hand, the 1st time that a simple private has touched the hand of his sovereign . . . I am proud of it.'

A NEW YACHT AND A TITLE

During the war, the royal family went to France, to visit the emperor Napoleon III. They crossed the Channel in the new royal yacht, *Victoria and Albert.*

The queen's last child, Princess Beatrice, was born in 1857. Albert was finally given his own title, Prince Consort – but it came by order of the queen herself, not from parliament.

▲ **The descendants of Queen Victoria and Prince Albert. There were 37 great-grandchildren living at Victoria's death.**

THE FAMILY PHOTOGRAPH

In 1858, Vicky, the Princess Royal, married Crown Prince Frederick William of Prussia. The queen was pleased, and afterwards wrote to her daughter every day. At the wedding, the *Wedding March* by Felix Mendelssohn was played – as it has been at countless weddings since. There were wedding photographs. Everyone had to stay very still while the photographer exposed a glass plate in the camera.

THE DEATH OF ALBERT

IN 1857, VICTORIA was saddened to hear of fighting in India. The British East India Company used troops to put down an uprising that had begun among Indian soldiers. After the fighting, which the British called the Indian Mutiny, much of India passed into the control of the British government. It became part of the British empire.

ALBERT'S ILLNESS

Victoria was healthier than Albert. She was rarely ill and disliked 'overheated' rooms, while he complained of the cold, and sometimes wore a wig to keep his bald head warm. He worked too hard and he worried about the Prince of Wales. The prince's behaviour shocked his upright father. Albert heard news of his son, now with the army, gambling and having an affair with an actress. His parents were looking forward to his planned marriage to Princess Alexandra of Denmark.

▲ Prince Albert in 1861. He was overworked, in poor health and depressed by the behaviour of the Prince of Wales.

EVENTS

1857 Indian Mutiny.
1858 Brunel's ship Great Eastern, *the biggest ever built, sails across the Atlantic for the first time.*
1859 Victoria's first grandchild is born. He grows up to be Kaiser (emperor) William II of Germany. Charles Darwin's ideas on evolution cause conflict between the church and scientists.
1860 French and British troops enter Peking (Beijing), China's capital.
1861 Start of American Civil War. Victoria's mother dies. Prince Albert dies. Victor Emmanuel is first king of united Italy.

In November 1861, Albert fell ill with typhoid fever, probably as a result of contaminated water. Though desperately ill, Albert went on working at his desk. One of his last acts helped to keep Britain from taking sides in the American Civil War between the Northern and Southern states. A Northern warship stopped a British vessel, and there was a risk of war. Albert rewrote a government message to the North, making it more polite. Finally, worn out, he died on 14 December.

A QUEEN ALONE

The queen was lost without Albert to guide and advise her. She had relied on his help even to choose a bonnet. Alone, she was rather shy and nervous. Albert had kept her calm when she was angry, and had shown her that change could be good. In her misery, she hid from the world. Albert's clothes were laid out each evening, with hot water and a clean towel – as if he were still alive. The queen blamed the Prince of Wales for Albert's death. She refused to let the prince share in the work she must now do alone.

▲ Queen Victoria in 1861, the year of Albert's death. Shocked and grieving, she shunned public life for five years.

BRITISH INDIA

By the early 1800s, the British East India Company controlled much of India. It was more interested in trade than in changing the way Indians lived. But in 1857, soldiers in northern India revolted. One cause of the trouble was the use of a new rifle cartridge with a wrapping which a soldier bit off before firing. Indian soldiers believed the cartridge was greased with the fat of cows and pigs. This offended Hindus and Muslims. Towns were attacked and British people killed. The British sent fresh troops and many Indians died in the fighting before the rebellion – known as the Indian Mutiny – ended. In 1858, the British government took control of British-ruled India. The picture shows British troops storming Delhi.

▼ This cartoon, entitled 'A Court of King Cholera', drew attention to the squalor and poverty of the districts where the disease reigned.

▲ The Albert Memorial was erected in London's Hyde Park. The prince's statue shows him holding a copy of the catalogue to the Great Exhibition.

◾ WIDOW ◾

ALBERT'S TOMB AT Windsor became a shrine. The queen often visited it to gaze at his marble statue. She refused to return to public duties, although the government urged her to show herself. It was three years after Albert died before she could bring herself to ride in an open carriage. She kept busy seeing to state papers, and worrying over her growing family and politics.

▲ Prime minister William Gladstone was a liberal, reforming statesman but Victoria found him hard to like.

▼ Queen Victoria at Osborne with her Highland servant John Brown.

TRUSTY JOHN BROWN

In 1865, Victoria was told of the death of Lord Palmerston. A bold prime minister, he had made Britain respected (and disliked) abroad. Victoria felt no loss. 'I never liked him,' she wrote. But the death of her uncle Leopold, a friend from childhood, made her very sad. Feeling even more alone, she turned for companionship to a loyal servant called John Brown. A gruff Scot, Brown had gone deer-hunting with Albert at Balmoral.

EVENTS

1863 *Marriage of the Prince of Wales to Princess Alexandra. In the US Civil War, the Northern army wins the battle of Gettysburg.*
1864 *The Italian leader Garibaldi receives a hero's welcome in Britain.*
1865 *President Abraham Lincoln of the USA is shot and killed. Lewis Carroll's* Alice in Wonderland *is published.*
1866 *Swedish chemist Alfred Nobel invents a new explosive called dynamite. The first telegraph cable across the Atlantic Ocean links Europe and America.*
1867 *Victoria lays the foundation stone for the Albert Hall in London. The typewriter is invented. Miners seek diamonds in South Africa. Canada becomes a self-governing dominion.*
1868 *Disraeli becomes prime minister. Victoria holidays in Switzerland and climbs on a glacier.*

THE WORKHOUSE

FOR HUNDREDS of years, looking after the poor had been the job of the local church and parish. The government passed a law, the Poor Law, to enforce this arrangement. Parishes had to find work for the poor. They also built workhouses to provide food and shelter for the old, sick and orphaned. Workhouses were inhospitable places, often harshly run, with separate quarters for men and women. Even old married couples were parted if poverty forced them into the workhouse. Every aspect of life, including mealtimes, was regimented.

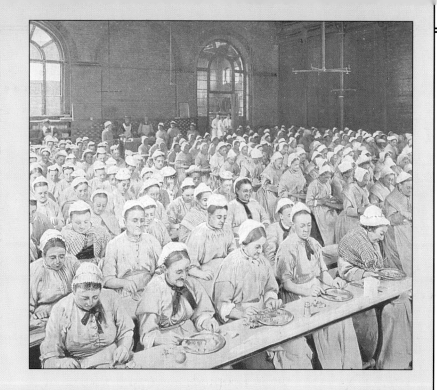

▼ The queen with her prime minister, Benjamin Disraeli. She enjoyed his company and supported his policy of strengthening Britain's position in the world and expanding the empire.

CHANGE

In 1866, the queen opened parliament for the first time since Albert's death. She dressed in black, the colour of mourning, which she wore for the rest of her life.

Many working people were calling for reform, so that they could vote in elections. Only some men in Britain had the right to vote and no women at all. Victoria feared disturbances from the crowds with their banners and protests. They might lead to violent revolution, as in France.

The queen was not against change. In fact, she had more respect for the hardworking poor than for the idle rich with whom her son Bertie enjoyed himself.

TWO GREAT PRIME MINISTERS

The queen's favourite prime minister at this time was Benjamin Disraeli. He was a witty man who wrote novels and made his reports on government business entertaining to read. He had also helped raise money to build the Albert Memorial in London.

Disraeli's great rival, William Ewart Gladstone, had complained of the cost of the memorial to Albert. Victoria never liked Gladstone. As prime minister, he talked endlessly and gave her long, dull papers to study. Disraeli was far more exciting, with his vision of an ever-growing British empire that had Victoria as its sovereign.

■ EMPRESS OF INDIA ■

GOODS PASSED BETWEEN India and Britain by a sea route round Africa. The building of the Suez Canal to link the Red Sea and the Mediterranean shortened the voyage by nearly 10,000 kilometres. Disraeli helped Britain to buy a controlling share in the canal, which opened in 1869. It was big enough for large steamships and cut the journey time to the East by weeks. India held a fascination for the queen, so she was delighted to become Empress of India in 1876.

WAR IN EUROPE

With so many of her children married into royal families across Europe, the queen found the idea of any war worrying. New guns and explosives were making wars more terrible. Prussia and France fought in 1871. Prussia's victory meant that Victoria's grandson William would one day be emperor of a new united Germany.

HAPPIEST AT HOME

Victoria's many grandchildren came on visits. The children spent hours with 'Gangan', one at a time, in her room. The queen seldom went out, though she did visit hospitals and

EVENTS

1869 Suez Canal opens. The first railway across the United States is completed.
1870 Charles Dickens dies. Lehzen, the queen's old governess, dies.
1871 France becomes a republic. Stanley and Livingstone meet in Africa.
1876 Victoria is declared Empress of India. The telephone is invented.
1877 Edison invents a machine that records and plays back sounds.
1879 The electric light bulb is invented.
1880 Frozen meat from Australia goes on sale in Britain.
1883 Death of John Brown, the queen's servant.
1884 Death of Victoria's son Leopold, who suffered from haemophilia.
1885 German engineers Daimler and Benz invent the motor car.

BRITAIN AND AFRICA

As head of the largest empire in history, the queen took a keen interest in Africa. She followed the adventures of explorers such as Livingstone and Stanley, and of her generals Gordon and Kitchener fighting in the Sudan. She heard news of diamond mines in South Africa and the empire-building plans of Cecil Rhodes. Britain had led the 'scramble for Africa', as European nations seized colonies. The picture shows the fatal attack on General Gordon at Khartoum in 1885.

▲ Four generations: the queen with her son (later Edward VII), her grandson (later George V) and great grandson (the Duke of Cornwall).

◄ A procession of ships at the opening of the Suez Canal in 1869. The canal was built by the French, though the British derived more benefit from it.

distribute medals to brave soldiers and sailors. Privately she amused herself by singing cheerful Gilbert and Sullivan songs with her ladies in waiting. She also knitted quilts and wrote her diaries, publishing some of them as *Leaves from a Journal of Our Life in the Highlands*.

Victoria's desire not to show herself in public was partly understandable. In 1882, there was another attempt on her life – the seventh. There was trouble in Ireland, with murders and bombings, and the queen was a possible terrorist target.

TROUBLES IN IRELAND

Ever since the famines of the 1840s, Ireland's troubles had grown. The Fenian Brotherhood fought for independence from Britain. In parliament, Charles Stewart Parnell argued for Irish self-government – Home Rule. Gladstone put forward a proposal for Home Rule in 1886, but it was defeated. He tried once more in 1893, but again failed.

SO MANY CHANGES

The world was changing fast. People could send a telegraph message under the sea from Britain to the United States. Americans could travel by train from one side of their huge country to the other.

In 1878, Professor Bell came to show the queen his amazing new invention, the telephone. In the mid-1880s, she learned with astonishment that in Germany people were driving about in 'horseless carriages'. Some people predicted that soon travellers would fly across the oceans! Where would all this progress lead?

◀ Victoria at Balmoral with her Hindu secretary – the Munshi. He was one of many Indian servants.

▼ Queen Victoria invests the sultan of the Ottoman empire with the Order of the Garter on board the Royal Yacht on 17 July 1867.

■ THE VICTORIAN AGE ■

THE LAST YEARS of Victoria's life saw a number of great parades and processions. In 1886, she opened parliament for the last time, helped up the steps by her daughter. Gladstone was still trying to solve the Irish question; his rival in parliament was the Conservative Lord Salisbury, who was three times prime minister.

EVENTS

1887 *Golden Jubilee. Victoria gains Indian servants and learns some Hindustani to talk to them. One servant, the Munshi, acts as her faithful helper and adviser.*
1888 *Grandson Kaiser William II becomes emperor of Germany.*
1893 *Women in New Zealand get the vote.*
1895 *Discovery of X-rays.*
1896 *The first modern Olympic Games are held at Athens, Greece.*
1897 *Victoria's Diamond Jubilee*
1898 *Gladstone dies.*
1899 *Victoria's last trip abroad, holidaying in Italy and the south of France. Start of the Boer War in South Africa. The queen orders 100,000 tins of chocolate to be sent to the soldiers.*
1900 *Siege of Ladysmith (South Africa) is lifted by British army. Victoria drives through London's cheering crowds. She wears glasses in public, for her eyesight is fading.*
1901 *Six states of Australia unite as a commonwealth. US President McKinley is shot dead. Queen Victoria dies. Edward VII becomes king.*

JUBILEES

In 1887, the queen celebrated her Golden Jubilee, marking 50 years of her reign. Lucky prisoners all over the empire were freed, except those found guilty of cruelty to animals – 'one of the worst traits in human nature' thought the queen. Messages and poems of congratulation came from all around the world. For the jubilee, she rode in a carriage through London wearing a lace bonnet with diamonds. She refused to wear a crown and robes. Jubilee coins and medals were given out and 30,000 children in Hyde Park received a bun, milk and a jubilee mug. A huge balloon rose into the sky. 'Look, there's Queen Victoria going to heaven!' shouted one child.

In 1897 came the Diamond Jubilee. Victoria had reigned longer than her grandfather, George III – and therefore longer than any other

▲ Bombay railway station, an imperial monument in India.

NEW ELECTRIC AGE

The queen enjoyed many of the new inventions, such as the 'gramophone' machine on which she made a recording of her own voice. For her Diamond Jubilee, London's streets sparkled with decorations – thousands of tiny gas jets mingled with electric light bulbs. Her reign had begun with gas and was ending with electricity – symbol of a new age.

▼ The Diamond Jubilee procession, a time for national rejoicing.

▼ 'Just in time' – a Victorian pillar box.

▼ A magic lantern slide of the queen at her Diamond Jubilee, 1897.

British monarch. This time the carriage procession stopped outside St Paul's Cathedral for a short service of thanksgiving. The queen pressed a button to send a telegraph message around the empire: 'From my heart I thank my beloved people. May God bless them!' She was now frail and appeared on the balcony at Buckingham Palace in her wheelchair. The next great procession would be her funeral, and the queen had her own ideas about that.

END OF AN ERA

The queen died at Osborne, surrounded by her family. Her coffin was taken to London by train and people knelt in the fields as it steamed past. Many felt that they had lost the 'Mother of the Empire'. London's streets were hung with white and purple. The queen had wanted little pomp and no black: her coffin should travel on a gun carriage covered in flowers. She loved bright colours. As she had wished, she was laid to rest beside Albert in the light, bright Mausoleum at Frogmore near Windsor.

LEGACY

Victoria gave her name to the Victorian age. It was a time of great achievements in science and industry, and of great changes in the way people lived and worked. Victoria is remembered all over the world – through statues, street names, parks, cities, states, a waterfall and lake in Africa.

The Victorians left us many familiar landmarks, such as railway stations, town halls, parks, schools – even public lavatories, drinking fountains and letter boxes. They created the industrial age in which we live.

▲ A photograph of the queen's funeral procession passing through London. Thousands lined the route, openly weeping.

▶ The monument to Queen Victoria outside Buckingham Palace in London. The inscription reads: Regina Imperatrix (Queen Empress).

■ GLOSSARY ■

ANAESTHETIC Substance that makes a person feel no pain.

BOER South African settler descended from the Dutch. Britain fought a war against the Boers from 1899 to 1902.

CHARTIST A supporter of a movement to extend political power to the working class. The name comes from the 'People's Charter', which called for voting in secret for all men over 21.

CHOLERA An infectious, often fatal, disease caused by bacteria. The provision of fresh, clean drinking water during Victorian times helped to rid Britain of the disease.

CONSERVATIVE One of the two major political parties in Victorian times (and today). Peel and Disraeli were two of Victoria's Conservative prime ministers.

CO-OPERATIVE Society whose members share the profits from the distribution and sale of goods, mostly through shops.

COURT The palace of a king or queen and the people who attend the monarch.

CRIMEA Peninsula on the Black Sea in what is now Ukraine, where a three-year war against Russia was fought and won by Britain, France, Turkey and Sardinia.

EMPEROR/EMPRESS The male or female ruler of an empire. The wife of an emperor is also called empress.

EMPIRE A group of nations or states under the rule of a single person.

FAMILY TREE Chart showing relationships and lines of descent of a family.

FAMINE Period when food is so scarce in an area that people starve to death.

FENIAN A member of an association of Irishmen devoted to the overthrow of the British government in Ireland.

FURNACE A closed apparatus in which fuel is burned to create very high temperatures in order, for example, to smelt iron.

GOVERNESS A female teacher in a private household.

HOME RULE Policy of self-government for the Irish.

JUBILEE A special anniversary, especially a 50th.

KALEIDOSCOPE A toy consisting of a tube with mirrors in which an array of coloured shapes can be shaken into ever-changing symmetrical patterns.

LIBERAL One of two major political parties in Victorian times. Gladstone was one of its prime ministers.

LORD CHAMBERLAIN The person who runs the royal household.

LUNATIC ASYLUM Term formerly used for a mental hospital or home.

MAUSOLEUM A large, elaborate tomb.

MINISTER A senior member of the government, responsible for a department.

MONARCHY A system of government in which the head of state is a king or queen. In a constitutional monarchy, the head of state is a king or queen, but power is in the hands of the government and parliament.

MUTINY Open revolt by sailors or soldiers against their commanding officers.

PARISH A district attached to a church and looked after by a priest or minister, or a local government district.

PARLIAMENT An elected assembly of representatives who make laws for a country.

PRIME MINISTER The chief minister and head of the government.

PRINCE CONSORT A prince who is the husband of a reigning queen.

PRINCE REGENT A prince who rules on behalf of a sovereign who is too ill or too young to rule.

PRIVY COUNCILLORS A monarch's private advisers. Nowadays these positions are held by government ministers.

RAGGED SCHOOL A school that gave free lessons to poor 'ragged' children.

SMALLPOX A generally fatal infectious disease caused by a virus. Vaccination has completely eradicated the disease.

SULTAN A Muslim king or ruler.

TELEGRAPH Communication using coded electrical signals sent through a line connected to transmitting and receiving instruments.

TUBERCULOSIS Disease of the lungs, also known as consumption, that killed many people in Victorian times, but which can be treated today.

TYPHOID An infectious disease that causes a high fever and was mostly fatal during Victorian times.

VACCINATE To inoculate or administer a vaccine that gives immunity to a disease such as smallpox.

WATERLOO Place in Belgium where the last battle of the Napoleonic wars was fought, in which Napoleon was defeated by Britain and her allies.

WORKHOUSE A place where the poor could live in return for working.

PLACES TO VISIT

Kensington Palace,
London.
Victoria's birthplace.

Buckingham Palace,
London.
Victoria's home as queen.

Windsor Castle and Great Park,
Berkshire.
Victoria's home. Albert died here. Albert Memorial Chapel.

Frogmore,
Home Park, Windsor.
Home of Victoria's mother for 21 years. Her mausoleum and that of Victoria and Albert.

Osborne House,
Isle of Wight.
Holiday home of Victoria and Albert. Where Victoria died. Royal apartments and nursery suite open to view, plus Swiss Cottage and Museum in grounds.

Museum of London.
Collections of Victoriana.

National Railway Museum,
York.
Queen Victoria's saloon from the royal train.

Victoria and Albert Museum,
South Kensington, London.
Built with money from the 1851 Great Exhibition. Victoria laid the foundation stone of the present building in 1899.

Albert Memorial,
Kensington Gardens, London.
Completed 1876.

Balmoral Castle,
Scotland.
Holiday home of Victoria and Albert.

■ INDEX ■

A

Albert, Prince 4, 12-13, *12, 13*, 17, 18, *22*
   advice to Victoria 14, 16
   first visit to England 11
   illness and death 22-23
   title 13, 21
Albert Memorial *23*, 25, 31
Alexandra of Denmark, Princess 22
Anaesthetics 16

B

Balaclava, battle of *20-21*
Balmoral, Scotland 5, 17, 27, 31
Beatrice, Princess 21
Bell, Alexander Graham 27
Black Country *19*
Bombay railway station *28-29*
British East India Company 22, 23
British empire *4-5*
   Africa 26
   India 23, 26, *28-29*
Brontë, Charlotte 17
Brown, John 24, *24*
Buckingham Palace 11, 15, 16, 31

C

Canterbury, archbishop of 11, *10-11*
Chartists *12*, 13, 16-17
Cholera 15, 16, *23*
Christmas *14*, 15
Civil War, American 23
Cleanliness and Godliness 15, *15*
Co-operative shop 13
Conroy, Sir John 8, 11
Cornwall, Duke of *26*
Crimean War 20-21, *20-21*
Crystal Palace 18, *18*

D

'Dame schools' 8
Delhi, storming of *22-23*
Diamond Jubilee 28-29, *28-29*
Diamonds: Koh-i-Noor 18
   mining 26
Dickens, Charles: *Nicholas Nickleby* 8
   Oliver Twist 10, 12
Diseases 14-15
   see also Cholera; Typhoid fever
Disraeli, Benjamin 25, *25,* 26

E

Edward VII, king *26*
Empress of India 26
Ernest (Victoria's cousin) 11
Family life: 'royal family' 5, 14-15, *14-15*, 16, 17
   size of families 14-15, *14-15*

F

Fenian Brotherhood 27
Feodore (Victoria's sister) 9
Fire service 19
Frederick William, Crown Prince of Prussia 21

G

Gaslight 15, *15*
George III, king 6, 28
George IV, king 4, 6, 9
George V, king *26*
Gladstone, William Ewart *24*, 25, 27, 28
Golden Jubilee 28
Gordon, General 26, *27*
Government, British system of 13, 14
Gramophone 28
Great Exhibition 18-19, *18, 19*

H

Helena, Princess 15
Holidays 9, 16, 17, *16-17*
Home Rule 27
'Horseless carriages' 27
Hospitals 19

I

Indian Mutiny 22, 23, *22-23*
Inventions 15, *15*, 27, 28, *29*
Ireland: potato famine *12-13*, 13, 16
   self-government question 27, 28

J

Jenner, Dr Edward 7

K

Kensington Palace, London 6, 7, 8, 31
Kent, Duchess of 6, 7, *12*
Kent, Edward Duke of 6, *6*
Kitchen, ideal *18*
Kitchener, General 26

L

Leaves from a Journal of Our Life in the Highlands 27
Lehzen (Victoria's governess) 8, 9, 14
Leopold, king of the Belgians 9, 24
Light Brigade, charge of the *20-21*
Livingstone, David 26
Lord chamberlain *10-11*
Louise, Princess 16

M

Mausoleum, Frogmore 24, 29, 31
Melbourne, Lord 11, 12
Mendelssohn, Felix: *Wedding March* 21
Millais, John 14
Munshi, the *27*, 28

N

Newspaper reporting 20
Nightingale, Florence 20-21
Nursing, development of 20-21, *20-21*

O

Osborne House 16, 17, *16-17, 24*, 29, 31

P

Paddington Station *16*
Palmerston, Lord 11, 24
Parliament, opening of 25, 28
Parnell, Charles Stewart 27
Paxton, Joseph 18
Peel, Sir Robert 11, *12*, 14, 16
'Penny black' *12*
Pets 10, 11, 13
Photography: family wedding 21
   war 20
Police service 19
Pollution, industrial *19*
Poor Law 25
Population, increase in 19
Prime ministers 11, 14, 24, *24*, 25, *25*
Prince Consort 21
Privy councillors 11

R

Ragged schools 8
Railways 16-17, *16*
Rhodes, Cecil 26
Riots, workers *12*, 13
Royal tours 10
Royal yacht 21, *27*

S

Safety matches 15
Safety pins 15
Sanitation, improvements to 16
Schools 8, *9*, 19
   first for nurses 21
'Scramble for Africa' 26
Stanley, Henry Morton 26
Stockton and Darlington railway 16
Strikes 13
Suez Canal 26, *26*
Sultan of the Ottoman empire *27*
Sunday school 8

T

Telegraph messages: Diamond Jubilee 29
   transatlantic 27
Telephone 27
Toys 9, *9*
Typhoid fever 11, 15, 23

V

Victoria, Princess (Princess Royal) 14, 21
Victoria, queen *13, 23*, 25, *25*, 27
   accession *10-11*, 11
   assassination attempts 14, 27
   childhood 7, 8-9, *9*
   children 5, 14-15, *14-15*, 16, 21
   coronation *10-11*, 11
   death of 29, *29*
   descendants *21*, 26, *26*
   Jubilees 28-29, *28-29*
   marriage 12-13
   mourning for Albert 23, 24
   public duties 7, 10, 18, 21, 26-27, *27*
   signature *4*
Victoria and Albert (royal yacht) 21, *27*
Victoria Monument *29*
Voting rights 25

W

Wales, Prince of (Albert Edward) 14, 22
Wellington, Duke of 11, *12*
William IV, king 4, 11
Windsor Castle 9, 16, 31
Winterhalter, Franz Xavier, portrait by *4*
Workhouse 25, *25*
Working class 10, 13
   'ideal homes' 18, *18*